How to Train Goldfish Using Dolphin Training Techniques

C. Scott Johnson

VANTAGE PRESS
New York

FIRST EDITION

Copyright © 1995 by C. Scott Johnson

Published by Vantage Press, Inc.
516 West 34th Street, New York, New York 10001

Manufactured in the United States of America
ISBN: 0-533-11292-3

0 9 8 7 6 5 4 3 2 1

Contents

Preface

When I told my friends that I was writing a book about how to train goldfish, they, except for my friends who are animal trainers, thought I was kidding. "I didn't know goldfish could be trained; I thought they were too dumb," was their usual comment. What they didn't know is that intelligence and trainability are two different things. Today everything from insects to elephants is being trained using a technique behaviorists call "operant conditioning," which is described in this book. Operant conditioning is a training method that makes use of positive —in this case food—rewards, and punishment is never used.

In the more than thirty years I have been involved with animal training and animal trainers, I have found that there is a great deal of interest among young people, and older people too, in how animals, and more specifically dolphins, are trained. Few people have the opportunity to train dolphins, and those who do usually are experienced trainers. Having been involved in U.S. Navy projects in which nurse sharks were trained to do some simple behaviors such as retrieve rings, it occurred to me that goldfish would be a good animal for aspiring trainers to practice with. They are readily available, easy to keep, and not too expensive. The following procedures are ones I developed while training two goldfish of my own.

Animal training, even training goldfish, can be a very frustrating experience, and not everyone has the temperament and patience to succeed. If you are easily discouraged and have a temper that is easily aroused, training goldfish is probably something you would be better forgoing.

The book is not very long and it is recommended that you read it completely through before you start buying aquariums and fish.

How to Train Goldfish Using Dolphin Training Techniques

1
The Fish Tank

Before you buy a fish, you need to get your aquarium set up. It is extremely important that you provide a good home for your fish to live in. For a five-inch fish, the aquarium should have a volume of at least ten gallons, following the rule of one or more gallons per inch of fish length. Tanks or bowls smaller than ten gallons are too small to use for training. The tank must be outfitted with good aeration, filtration, and temperature control to keep the water purified and heated. There are several good books on what is required to provide your fish a healthy home, and the people at the aquarium store are always happy to help you with your fish's aquarium needs. The importance of having a good home for your fish cannot be overemphasized.

The tank will need a top cover. These are available, as are all your tank needs, at any good aquarium store or pet shop. Most tank covers have lights in them and lids that open for feeding. Since you will be training your fish from the top of the tank, you will need a cover that can be completely removed for your training sessions with the fish.

Tank location is very important. It should be put in a room where there is not much traffic, and the temperature should not vary greatly throughout the day and night. Ideally, the only person to regularly come near the tank should be you.

If you have a pet cat, be sure it cannot bother your fish. A frightened fish is impossible to work with. Once you have installed the tank and are sure that the water is well aged and free from any harmful chemicals that may be in your drinking water, you are ready to begin looking for a suitable fish.

2
Choosing the Right Fish

Choosing the right fish is very important. Fish, like dogs, people, and other animals, are all different from one another. Each one has its own personality, fears, and other hang-ups. There are variations between fish species as well as variations between fish of the same species. Since our objective is to learn how to train fish, it is important that we pick a fish that will make our task as easy as possible. I use the singular in referring to fish because only one fish can be trained at a time and it must have its own private tank.

My personal choices are the fantail goldfish or the common Japanese goldfish (the Wakin). Koi are not recommended because they grow too large for reasonable-sized aquariums. Telescope-eyed and celestial goldfish are not recommended because they may injure their protruding eyes on some of the training props that will be used.

Fish size is very important. The larger the goldfish the better. A four- or five-inch-long fantail is ideal. Larger fish eat more than smaller fish, and since a food-reward system is used in training, the more they can eat the better. A large fantail can cost $25 or more depending on its color pattern.

For choosing a fish for training, its color pattern is of no importance. The most important consideration is how well the fish is adapted to its environment, its tank. It should not be easily frightened and run away when its tank is approached. On the contrary, a good fish to choose is one that comes to the side of the tank when you approach it. You want a fish that hurries

2

to the spot where food is put into the tank and feeds. And the fish should, of course, be in good health.

Do not be in a hurry to purchase a fish; the time making a good selection will amply be repaid in the training time you gain later on. Go to as many shops as you can before making a selection. When you look at fish in a pet shop or aquarium store, examine them carefully for any sign of injury or illness. If you hold a finger against the aquarium, it's a good sign if the fish comes over and nibbles at the glass next to your finger. Some aquariums don't like for you to do this because it smudges the glass, so be sure to ask if it's all right. Also, ask someone at the store to put a little food in the tank to see how the fish reacts. It should readily come over to the food and eat.

3

The Training Method

The general training method we will use is the same as that used to train dolphins, whales, sea lions, and most other birds and animals. This method is called operant conditioning, which means we are going to condition the fish to operate in a chosen way, such as swimming through a ring. Operant conditioning works by rewarding the fish with bits of food when it performs correctly and withholding food when it does not. Punishment is *never, never* used. Punishment only makes the fish afraid of you, which is the opposite of what you want.

It is important that only one person train the fish, especially in the early learning stages. Different people behave and react differently, and fish may become confused if they are exposed to more than one training technique.

It is also very important that you keep good records of everything you do with the fish. All good professional trainers keep notes on the progress of their training programs with animals. So get a notebook in which to record all the events of your training procedure. Some of the things that are important to record are: date and time of training session, water temperature, description of training procedure, fish behavior, amount of food fed, and time spent in session. The reason that it is so important to keep good records is that it is impossible to remember from day to day what you did and how the fish behaved. Sure, you can probably remember what you did yesterday, but how about last week or last month? These records are vital to determining how much the fish is improving and when it is safe to move on to the next stage of training. From time to time, it will be necessary to add water or to change part of the water in the fish's tank. Be sure to note this or any other change in or around the aquarium. Such changes may have an effect on the fish's behavior, and you need to know if behavioral changes are due to something you have done or if the fish is getting sick and needs medical attention.

Start recording your progress from the very beginning. You should record where and when you bought your fish and aquarium, how long you aged the aquarium's water before introducing the fish to it, along with water temperature and the results of any water tests you have made.

4

Initial Training

The type of food you use is very important. In training dolphins, individual small fish are used to reward the animal during training. You will want to use individual pieces of food to feed your fish during training. Powder or flake food will not do because you can't handle it very easily and it takes the fish too long to find and eat it. The Nippon Pet Food Company makes a food that works very well. It is their basic floating-type food and comes in small spherical pieces about the size of a BB shot. For ease of handling, I pour several of the BB's into a paper saucer or bowl so that they can be picked up one at a time.

With your fish established in its aquarium and the water temperature stabilized, it's time to start your training schedule. In the beginning, you want to get the fish used to your presence and to associate you with the food and being fed. Three or four times a day, take off the top of the aquarium and feed the fish a small amount of food. Remain by the tank until the fish has eaten, which should only be a few minutes. Always feed from the same position at one end of the tank. This will be the position you use during all of the training and should not be changed. In the beginning, if the fish is shy of your presence, use a little flaked food to get the fish's attention. Sprinkle a few flakes at the end of the tank, and stir it up with your finger or a small stick. This will cause some of the flakes to dissolve, and the fish will smell or taste it and soon find the flakes on the surface. Cover the end of the tank that you work from with a piece of paper. If you don't do this, the fish will be distracted by your hand movements outside the tank. This feeding should be repeated three or four times a day.

If you have to go to work or school, feed the fish before leaving and then two or three times after you come home. Allow about an hour or so between feedings. Do not overfeed. Fish, being cold-blooded, do not need much food, and if you feed them too much, it is difficult to keep their attention. Remember, food is the only way you have of controlling what you want the fish to do.

Food is not as important to dolphins as it is to fish. That's why dolphins are more difficult to train than fish. Reducing the amount of food a dolphin gets has very little effect on its behavior, so you have to be very clever to get them to do what you want. Dolphins have what is called a low "hunger drive," and it's not possible to starve them into doing something they don't want to do. It's not possible to starve fish into doing something they don't want to do either. Sea lions are much more interested in food, and they are much quicker and easier to train. Under federal law, all dolphins, sea lions, and other marine mammals held in captivity must be offered food every day to prevent unskilled trainers from starving the animals and endangering their health.

Fortunately, fish are very hardy and reducing the amount of food they get does them no harm. In fact one of the most frequent mistakes made by fish owners is overfeeding. If fish are given more than they can readily eat, the excess food can pollute the aquarium water and endanger the fish's health.

It should only take a few days before your fish has become accustomed to its new home and is coming to the end of the tank when the lid is removed. At this point, start feeding the food in individual pieces (figure 1). Give the fish a piece of food, wait a few seconds, and then give it another one, and so on. The fish may take one piece of food and swim away and not come back for the next piece. If this happens, close the lid and come back in an hour and try again. The fish will gradually become more accustomed to this method of feeding and tend to stay near your end of the tank. Stay at the tank only a few minutes at a time,

Figure 1. Hand-feeding fish.

no more than five minutes. In about a week, the fish should be pretty well used to you and the feeding routine. Only feed a five-inch-long goldfish six or eight pieces at each session three or four times a day. Feed smaller fish less. If the fish's behavior does not improve, reduce by one-half the amount you feed it.

How is record keeping coming along? Are you recording the times you feed the fish, how much you feed, and how the fish behaves? How about water temperature?

5

Reinforcement

We will be training the fish using food as a reward or reinforcement for its behavior. This means that when the fish behaves as we wish, we give it a piece of food. For example, in the preceding section, we were rewarding the fish with food for coming to the side of the tank when we were there. This type of reward system works well enough when the fish is close to you, but does not work as well when the fish is being trained to do something on the other side of the tank. For example, what if you want to train the fish to touch something on the other side of the tank and return to you for its reward? Because it gets its food from you it will be reluctant to leave you and the food supply.

To train the fish when it is not preforming a behavior close to you, we use what is called a "secondary reinforcer" or "bridging stimulus," simply referred to as a "bridge." These are fancy terms used by behaviorists to describe the use of a signal that tells the fish that it has performed correctly and will get a piece of food if it returns to you.

If you have seen a dolphin or sea lion show at Sea World or some other oceanarium, you have seen a bridge signal being used, but you probably didn't know it at the time. If you had watched closely, you would have seen that the dolphin trainer had a whistle on a line around his or her neck. This is usually a dog whistle, which makes a sound too high in frequency for humans to hear well, and you may not have noticed it being used, since you were probably watching the dolphin. Most dolphins and other marine mammals can hear frequencies much higher than we humans can, and dog whistles make a good bridge signal. When the dolphin performed correctly, say, made a jump in the middle of the tank, the trainer blew on the whistle and the dolphin swam over to receive its reward of fish from the trainer. At one time police whistles were used, but they distracted the audience's attention away from the show animals, so the "silent" dog whistle is now preferred.

So the bridge signal is a training aid, a simple means of communicating to the animal, "Yes, come and get your piece of food. You have performed correctly."

Now, what do we use for a bridge signal and how do we teach the fish what it means? We know that goldfish have very good hearing but they can't hear frequencies as high as we can, so that rules out dog whistles. Just about any toy horn (figure 2) or whistle will work, even a kazoo. Door buzzers work very well, but you will need to epoxy them to the side of the fish tank so that the sound is transmitted into the tank. To operate the buzzer, you will need a switch that you can control with your foot because as you get into the training, you will find that you need both hands a lot of the time. Whistles have the advantage that you can hold them in your mouth, leaving both hands free, while training. Once you have chosen a bridging signaler, don't change it during your training program; a different signaler may confuse the fish.

Introduce the bridge signal to the fish during your regular feeding sessions. When the fish comes to the side of the tank near you, sound the bridge, give the fish a piece of food, and repeat this procedure throughout the feeding session. After you have been using the bridge during feeding for about a week, you should be ready to teach the fish its first behavior. The fish will not have completely learned what the bridge signal means yet, but it will learn more quickly while being trained in specific behavior.

Are you keeping your records up-to-date? The best time to record your observations is right after a training session.

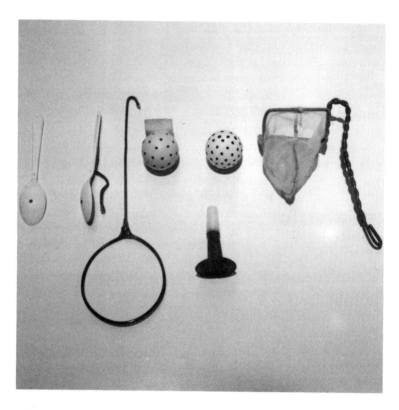

Figure 2. Props used for the first few behaviors. From left to right: spoon, spoon with wire clip, water-filled Ping-Pong ball with plastic foam float, hollow Ping-Pong ball, net. The red and white object below the hollow Ping-Pong ball is the toy horn used for a bridging stimulus.

6
Spoon Touching

Touching some object is often the first step in many animal-training programs. In the behaviorist's jargon, the object is often called a "manipulandon." In our case, the first manipulandon we will use is a simple plastic spoon, like the ones used on picnics (figure 2). There are many tricks used in animal training, and it will speed up the training here if we use one now. Paint a small spot about the size of the food pellets you are using on the center of the outwardly curved bowl of the spoon. You can use a black marking pen or any kind of waterproof black paint. We wish to trick the fish into thinking the dark spot on the spoon is a piece of food. This kind of deception is often used in training birds to peck at an object. In the case of birds, a piece of grain is glued to the manipulandon. Birds have much better eyes than fish and are harder to fool. There is only one rule in using tricks to train an animal: Never do anything that might harm the animal.

Now it's time to introduce the spoon with the fake food spot to the fish. With your bridge signal in your mouth ready to use, hold the spoon in one hand so that the spot is about an inch under water at your feeding station (figure 3). You should have a piece of food in your other hand. The fish will very likely swim over and bite at the spot. When this happens, sound the bridge, remove the spoon, and put a piece of food in the tank. As soon as the fish bites at the spot, it will know that it is not food and may behave in different ways. The worst thing that can happen is that the fish will be frightened and swim to the other side of the tank and stay there. If this happens, don't be discouraged.

Figure 3. Goldfish pushing (biting) on spoon.

Stop the training session, and go away for an hour or so before trying again.

The best thing that can happen is that the fish is not frightened and continues to bite at the spot. If this happens, continue bridging the fish, removing the spoon and offering food for four to six trials; then take a break of an hour or so before trying another four to six trials. Don't be surprised if the fish swims away from you and begins biting at its reflection in the tank windows or bites at floating bubbles. This is all new to the fish too, and it will be a little fearful and stressed.

You can expect this behavior from the fish every time you begin training something new. When the fish behaves this way, stop the session and walk away from the tank for a minute or two, then come back and try again. If the fish still ignores you, stop working for an hour or until the next day before you try again. Trainers call the short training breaks a "timeout." Timeouts are a very useful tool for trainers to use. Timeouts work because the fish is learning that you are the source of its food supply. When you leave, the food leaves; and when you return, its food returns too. It's important not to stay around the tank when the fish does not appear to want to work. Remember, you represent food to the fish, and while you are near, food is near. Don't let the fish train you to stay at the tank!

After an hour of timeout, the fish may come to your side of the tank but be reluctant to approach the spoon. To get the fish over its fear of the spoon, attach it to the side of the tank with a piece of tape or a wire bracket, as shown in the figure, so that the spot is below the surface of the water. Leave the spoon in the tank overnight. By the next day, the fish will have become used to the presence of the spoon and will no longer be afraid of it, but it won't be interested in touching it either. Begin by bridging and feeding the fish as you have in the past, but slowly bring the spoon close to the fish. If the fish doesn't start biting at the spoon on its own, gently touch the fish on the mouth with the spoon, sound the bridge, and give it a piece of food. After you begin touching the fish with the spoon, only then bridge and reward the fish for touching the spoon. Next hold the spoon

15

steady and reward the fish only when it touches the spoon. After bridging the animal, feed it and remove the spoon. Allow fifteen seconds to half a minute between trials. Keep the training sessions short so that the fish doesn't get too stressed; you can lengthen them as the fish gets accustomed to you and the training procedures. Don't overfeed the fish; six to eight pieces of food four times a day should be plenty.

These training sessions will require a lot of patience on your part. It will take about a week or so for the fish to start catching on to the idea that it has to bite the spoon to get a piece of food. There is a great deal of difference between individual fish, and some learn much quicker than others. Try to make things as easy for the fish as you can. One problem you will notice is that the fish can't see the food if it is placed directly in front of it. In the beginning, drop the food on one side or the other, an inch or so from one of its eyes. Even then they will often have trouble finding the food. If the fish and a floating piece of food get separated, hold the tip of your finger against the food so that it can be seen against your finger, and the fish will learn where to look. Eventually, with practice, you will be able to get the food directly in the fish's mouth by holding it underwater and letting the fish suck it from between your fingers. You will find that it is very helpful to have a towel nearby so you can dry your hands between trials. The food tends to stick to wet fingers when you try to pick it up.

How do you know when the fish has learned a behavior? The answer is that you don't. We know when the fish has performed what we want correctly or incorrectly, but the only way we have of getting the idea across to the fish is to continue training until the fish performs the trick consistently. Even when it appears that the fish has mastered a behavior, it is necessary to have it perform the operation from time to time to maintain the trick. An average fish should be touching the spoon pretty reliably in about two weeks after the touch training is started.

Once the fish is touching (biting) the spoon reliably at the position at the edge you have been using during the training so far, you can move the spoon a short distance to one side and train at the new location. By moving the spoon's location in small steps and then larger ones around the tank, the fish can be trained to find and touch the spoon at any location around the tank. Eventually, you can have the fish touch the spoon on one side of the tank, then move the spoon to the opposite side, then back again and so on, so that you have the fish swim back and forth from side to side of the tank to touch the spoon.

Are you keeping good records? How long did it take you to train the fish to touch the spoon reliably? Are you checking the water and changing part of it regularly as the tank-maintenance instructions recommend? Your fish's health is very important and should never be neglected.

7

Swimming through a Hoop

To train the fish to swim through a hoop, we make use of the spoon-touch training, but first we need a hoop. You can easily make a hoop out of a plastic-coated coat hanger like the one shown in figure 2. The hoop should be large enough for the fish to swim through easily; the one in the figure is about two and a half to three inches in diameter. It doesn't matter if the fish touches the hoop slightly with its fins. Coat the exposed ends of the hanger wire with epoxy or silicone tub caulk so they won't rust or scratch the fish.

We will need to fix the spoon so it can easily be hung from the top of the fish tank. An easy way to do this is to bend a piece of the plastic-coated coat hanger wire to form a bracket and epoxy it to the back of the spoon, as shown in figure 2. Again be sure to seal the ends of the wire so they don't rust.

To start training, hang the spoon from the top of the tank and hold the hoop in the tank so that it encircles the bowl of the spoon and is pressed up against the side of the aquarium (figure 4). The fish will see the hoop and may not want to touch the spoon. If this is the case, leave the hoop standing up in the tank overnight and continue training with the spoon-touch behavior.

By the next day, the fish's fear of the hoop should be reduced enough to start the spoon-in-hoop training again. If not, leave the hoop in the aquarium overnight again and don't work with the fish at all until the next day. By then the fish's hunger should overcome any remaining fear and it should touch the spoon in the hoop. From this point on, the hoop should not be left in the tank. After the fish is reliably touching the spoon, in a day or so,

18

Figure 4. Goldfish in hoop pushing on spoon.

move the hoop out from the side of the tank about half an inch and continue training, bridging the fish each time it touches the spoon.

Now what has to be done is to gradually move the hoop out farther and farther until the fish has to swim through the hoop to touch the spoon. If the fish is still somewhat fearful of the hoop, this may take two weeks or more and will require a great deal of patience on your part. The fish will also probably try to swim around the hoop and touch the spoon, but if it tries this, move the hoop in front of it so that it has to swim through it anyway. You may have to reduce the food ration by half and give the fish short (one minute) timeouts if it is reluctant to go through the hoop. But don't be in too big of a hurry. If it takes longer to train the behavior than you think it should, no harm is done. This will be your first good test to see if you have the temperament and patience to be an animal trainer.

Once the hoop is far enough away from the spoon so that the fish can easily swim between hoop and spoon, the fish can be bridged and fed before touching the spoon and the spoon can be eliminated after further training if you wish; the fish will be trained to swim through the hoop when you hold it in the tank. It may take a month or more to have the fish reliably going through the hoop in this way.

This can be a frustrating period of training. You may have to slowly move the hoop around so the fish has to swim through. Be very careful when you move the hoop so that you do not hit the fish and frighten it. It is a good sign when the fish starts biting and rubbing on the hoop. This means that it has associated the hoop with food, but it still doesn't understand that it has to swim through the hoop to be fed. Often the fish will swim under or around the hoop, but not through it, and come to the surface to be fed even though you haven't sounded the bridge. When this happens remove the hoop for ten or fifteen seconds and then put it back in the tank. It doesn't matter whether the fish swims through the hoop from left to right or right to left; sound the bridge and reward it each time it goes through the hoop. The fish will probably prefer one direction to go through.

20

Try to get the fish trained to swim through the hoop toward you. If you turn the hoop so that it is parallel with the long side of the tank, it doesn't matter which way it goes through. It will be helpful later in training the fish to retrieve the ring if it is in the habit of going through the hoop toward you or parallel to your side of the tank (figure 5).

By now the fish has learned that the food comes from your hand and any time one of your hands is near the top of the tank, the fish will be attracted to it, so you should keep your hands away from the tank unless you are feeding the fish. This is why you need to cover the tank window with a piece of paper so the fish can't see your hands through the glass. This problem happens with dolphins and most other animals that are trained using food rewards. If they can see the food or the hand you feed with, they will pay attention to your hand or the food and not to what you are training them to do. To the dolphin or fish, begging for food is easier than working for it.

After the fish has learned a trick, you really don't need to use the bridge signal anymore. The fish will know it has performed the behavior correctly when it sees your hand in the water with a piece of food and will come over to you to be fed. If it does not perform correctly, don't feed it and make the fish repeat the trick. If you are not strict enough in making the fish perform correctly, its behavior will degenerate into whatever the fish wants to do, and the fish will have trained you to feed it for doing whatever it wants to. On the other hand, if you are too hard on the fish, you may have trouble getting it to work at all. If, when you start a training session, the fish swims to the far side of the tank and faces away from you and won't respond to you, it may be letting you know that it is being worked too hard. If this happens it can be difficult to get it started working again. You can't starve the fish into responding, just like a dolphin. The problem is that, as hungry as the fish may be, it somehow considers what you are trying to get it to do as too difficult and it is under stress. The fish may also be easily startled. This is another sign of stress.

Fortunately, there is a simple way to get the fish out of its

Figure 5. Goldfish swimming through hoop.

bad mood and start working again. Take a few pieces of flake-type fish food and put them on the surface of the water. Stir the water near the flakes so some of them break up and sink. In a few seconds, the fish will detect the food in the water and begin swimming around, eating the flakes. Be ready with some of your regular training food, and feed the fish a piece or two. Then, using the spoon and hoop, have it do the behaviors that it has already mastered. It may be necessary to repeat this procedure at the beginning of several training sessions before the fish's behavior returns to normal. Do not ask too much of the fish until its behavior returns to normal; just train with the spoon and hoop and don't start the next behavior until it is working well again.

Now the fish has been trained to do two behaviors, touch the spoon and swim through the hoop. You can now connect the two behaviors together. First, put the hoop into the tank, and as the fish swims through it, hang the spoon on the side of the tank. The fish should swim over and push on the spoon. When it pushes the spoon, sound the bridge and feed the fish. You now have the fish doing two tricks for one food reward. Animal behaviorists call this "chaining" because one behavior leads to the next. This is how complicated series of behaviors are trained. The behaviors are broken down into a series of simple behaviors, and then they are chained together to produce a more compli-cated one.

To maintain the two tricks you have trained the fish to perform so far, you will need to have the fish perform them a few times daily, just as you have been doing with the spoon push. This will take some of your time away from training new behaviors; but fortunately the more the fish is trained, the quicker it learns new tricks. This is true of all animals. They gradually learn that they are expected to do something to be fed and become accustomed to the training environment.

Are you keeping good notes? Have you been checking the fish's water? You have invested a lot of time in your fish by now, and you don't want it to get sick because of your carelessness.

8

Ball Pushing

Compared to training the fish to swim through the hoop, training it to push a ball is easy. The order in which the various tricks are presented here is for a reason. The last trick in the series is retrieving a ring. This is the most difficult of the tricks to train, because a fish tends to be afraid of the ring, since the ring partially encloses its head as though it were being captured, and it must trust you to remove it. By the time we get to the ring-training procedure, both you and the fish will be much more familiar with each other and the fish will have greater trust in you. Any fear it might have had of the ring will be greatly reduced since it will have gone through the hoop many times, and the ring will not seem as great a threat as it would have if the ring-retrieval behavior had been trained earlier.

For this trick, the prop you will need is a ball that floats with its top just at the surface of the water. This can easily be done using a golf ball with a piece of foam plastic glued to the top so that it floats at the surface (figure 2). A second way to make the prop is to make a small hole in a Ping-Pong ball, fill it with water using an eyedropper, and seal the hole by gluing over it a piece of foam plastic so that it floats at the surface. A picture of the latter arrangement is shown in the picture. Covering the ball with painted dots will help get the fish to bump the ball as was done with the spoon in the first trick.

To begin training, place the ball in the center of the tank. The fish may come up and bump the ball right away (figure 6). If it does so, sound the bridge signal and feed it a piece of food. Then remove the ball, wait ten or fifteen seconds, and put the

Figure 6. Goldfish pushing water-filled Ping-Pong ball with plastic float.

ball in the tank again for the fish to touch. If the fish seems afraid of the ball, leave it in the tank overnight and remove it in the morning. Practice having the fish go through the hoop and push the spoon before trying to get it to touch the ball again. The fish's interest in the ball can sometimes be increased by touching the foam float gently with your finger. The fish by now will be starting to associate your hands with its food rewards and will probably swim up to the ball. If it still doesn't touch the ball, keep the ball at the side of the tank by holding the foam float. As with the spoon touch, push the ball against the fish's mouth if it doesn't quite touch the ball by itself. Bridge the fish and feed it as usual.

Now, to start with, reward the fish for touching the ball only once. After a day or so, only reward the fish for touching twice. Be sure to sound the bridge after each touch but only feed after the second. This can be continued for three and more touches, but before this can happen, the fish will usually start to push the ball rather than bump it. Since this is the desired behavior, reward the fish for pushing the ball greater and greater distances until the ball touches the side, any side, of the tank. You will find that the fish will have a tendency to push the ball again right after you sound the bridge. This is because the fish associates the ball with food and often bites the ball instead of coming to you for its reward.

Having the fish push the ball more than once before rewarding it is what behaviorists call putting the fish on a "ratio." The word "ratio" refers to the number of times the fish is required to do a behavior before it is rewarded. A ratio of three means that the fish must push the ball three times before it gets fed.

Don't be in too big of a hurry and push the fish too hard. It should take two to three weeks to train the ball-push trick.

You have now trained the fish to do three tricks. To maintain all the behaviors, they need to be practiced about once a day if possible. A good procedure is to have the fish do each trick twice each day during your last training session. If you chain swimming through the hoop and pushing on the spoon, you get two tricks for one reward, so you only use a total of four rewards to maintain the three behaviors. If the fish does not perform one of the tricks as well as it should, you might want to devote more time and rewards to that trick until it improves.

9
Basketball

For this trick you will need two props (figure 2). The first is an ordinary hollow Ping-Pong ball, nothing inside, that you have covered with painted dots so that at least one dot is showing underwater when the ball is floating on the surface. For the basketball net, buy the smallest dip net you can find at an aquarium store, or you may prefer to make your own. Using a pair of pliers, bend the wire in the net handle at the base of the net so that it is at right angles, as shown in the figure, to the net. Now bend a loop in the handle so that it clamps onto the side of the tank, as in the figure, so that the net can be adjusted up and down at the side of the tank. Also bend the side of the net facing the fish in a curve downward about a half of an inch. Next adjust the height of the net at the side of the tank so that the downward curved part of the net is just underwater enough so that the Ping-Pong ball will float easily into the net.

The fish will probably be a little frightened of the net, so be sure to attach the net to the wall of the tank the night before you start to train this new trick.

During the first basketball training session, place the Ping-Pong ball just outside the net so that when the fish pushes on it it will easily float into the net (figure 7). After several seconds the fish should come up and push on the ball. When it does, sound the bridge and give it a piece of food as usual. If the fish doesn't push on the ball fairly soon, remove the ball from the tank and wait a few seconds and replace it in the tank. It should not be long before the fish pushes on the ball. Because of the currents caused by the fish's swimming and the action of the filter system, the ball may not stay in the proper location but float away. To prevent this, either turn off your tank filter or hold the ball in position with your finger until the fish is almost touching it. If you turn the filter off, don't forget to turn it back on again when the training session is over.

After the fish has learned to push the ball into the net fairly reliably, raise the net until the ball won't quite float into the net. To get the ball into the net, the fish will have to push a little harder on the ball. After the fish is working well at this net height, raise it a little more and so on. Be careful not to move the net up so high that the fish can't push the ball into the net with relative ease. Move the ball out a few inches from the net so that the fish has to push the ball farther to get it into the net. If you position the net in the corner of the tank, as shown in the figure, the side of the tank will automatically help guide the ball into the net.

This may seem like a simple trick to train, but some fish have difficulty in learning that they need to push on the ball harder and harder to get it into the net. After the fish has been doing the behavior for several days and seems to be having difficulty getting the ball into the net at a certain height, it's best to lower the net to an easier height and move on to the next, and last, trick in this series. As you practice this behavior in your daily sessions, you can gradually raise the net height.

Are you keeping good notes and checking the aquarium's water quality frequently? You now have four behaviors to maintain, which means you have less time to train the fifth and last trick.

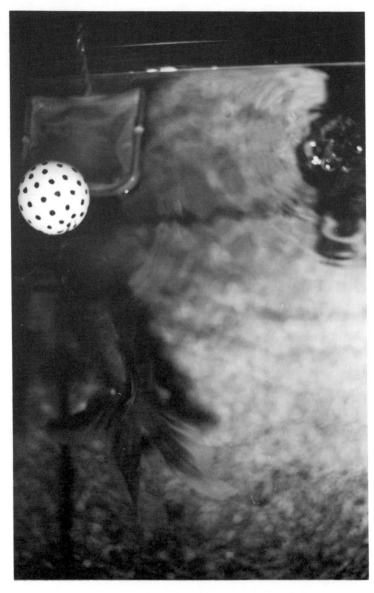

Figure 7. The fish is pushing the hollow Ping-Pong ball toward the net.

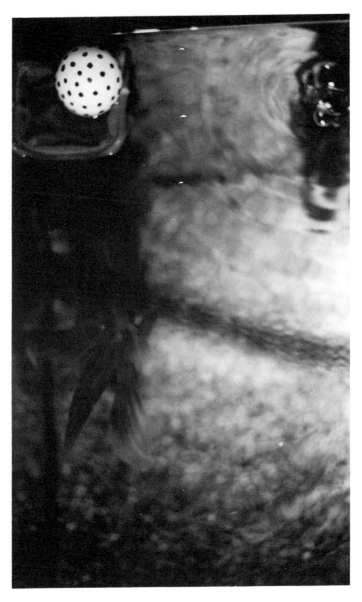

Figure 7a. Ball has been pushed into the net.

10
Ring Retrieval

Training the fish to retrieve a ring is done in several steps. The following training aids will be needed (see the figure). To begin with, make a hoop that is a little smaller than the one used in chapter 8 but large enough for the fish to swim through without difficulty. Attach a piece of plastic foam where the wire handle meets the hoop (figure 8). The purpose of this piece of foam is to make the hoop resemble the rings that will be used later.

Begin training using the hoop. You will probably expect the fish to swim through this hoop right away because it has already been trained to swim through a hoop, but you will probably be disappointed. With the addition of the piece of plastic foam, the hoop looks different to the fish than the hoop without flotation, and the hoop is smaller than the first hoop. The fish doesn't have a generalized concept of "hoop." A hoop that looks different to the one it's used to is a different object as far as it is concerned.

By now the fish has probably become so used to you giving it pieces of food that it ignores the sound of the bridge and watches your hands for its signal that it has performed correctly. In effect, your hand movements have become a visual bridge, so you have to be very careful that inadvertent hand movements don't distract or miscue the fish. The fish will also spend a good deal of time at the surface of the water begging and have little fear of your hands. You may be tempted to pet the fish with your finger, but you must never do so. The fish is covered with a coating of slime. This is the material that makes the fish slippery to handle, but it has a very important function. Fish slime protects the fish from harmful disease organisms, and if

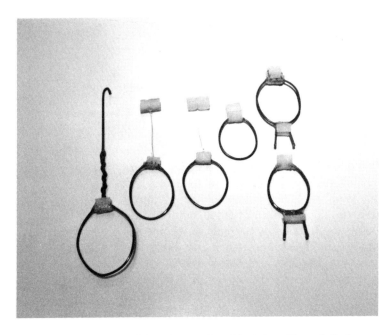

Figure 8. Props used for ring-retrieval training. From left: hoop with plastic foam, large ring with float attached, small ring with float attached, small floating ring, large sinking ring (above), small sinking ring.

the slime coat is damaged, these organisms are likely to attack the fish and make it sick. That's why all the props used in the tricks must be very smooth so they don't damage this coating. Start training in the same way you did with the hoop. With the spoon attached to the side of the tank, hold the new hoop with flotation in front as before. When the fish touches the spoon, sound the bridge and feed the fish. Gradually move the hoop away from the spoon until the fish swims all the way through the hoop to touch the spoon. Don't be in too big of a hurry, as with the hoop in chapter 8. It may take several training sessions and several days to get the fish to swim all the way through the new hoop. As before, once the hoop is moved far enough away from the spoon for the fish to swim around it and touch the spoon, it will probably try to do so. At this point, again as before, remove the spoon and, when the fish sticks its head into the hoop, put the spoon in the water to attract the fish to swim through the hoop to the spoon. It is helpful if you have the fish swim through the original hoop on every other trial.

When the fish is swimming through the hoop reliably, squeeze the sides of the hoop in so that the opening in the hoop is an oval about a half of an inch narrower than before. The fish will notice the change in the hoop's shape and will be reluctant to swim through. This kind of behavior will probably happen at each step of the procedure, but be patient. It will swim under and around, and push and bite the hoop or float, and do everything possible but swim through the hoop. It will also stick its head into the hoop and then back out, all these things it has done during the training in chapter 8. By now you should be good at sticking the spoon in the water just at the instant the fish has its head in the hoop to lure it through. You won't need the bridge signal anymore for training this behavior.

The next step is a big one. Once the fish is swimming through the narrowed hoop, make a ring that is slightly smaller than the hoop but still large enough for the fish to wiggle through. Attach a piece of plastic foam to the top of the ring (figure 8). The size of the foam piece should be just large enough so that the ring sinks slowly. You don't want the fish to have to carry any more weight than necessary. Tie one end of a piece of thread to the foam piece on the ring and the other end of the thread to a second, larger piece of foam. Adjust the length of the thread so that the ring will hang suspended in the middle of the tank.

One of the difficulties now encountered is that the ring is free-floating and will move about the tank. Start with the ring between you and the fish and about six inches or so from the end of the tank to make the fish's task as easy as possible. The fish will probably want to hang around you because you provide the food. You can easily move the fish to the other end of the tank by briefly holding the spoon or your finger in the water at the location you want it to go to, but don't let it touch the spoon. When you place the ring into the tank, be sure to remove your hand immediately because the fish will ignore the ring and come to the surface sucking (begging), expecting to get fed. If the fish pushes the ring to the side or it floats away, pick the ring up and start over. Again wait for the fish to stick its head into the ring; then show it the spoon so that it swims into the ring. Because of the size of the ring, the fish may swim all the way through, but that's all right. If the ring gets held up on its tail or fins, slip the ring on over the fish as it begs for its food reward at the end of the tank.

Never hurry when you are training. Alternate trials between the small hoop and the ring. Move slowly and deliberately, pausing fifteen to thirty seconds between trials. If the fish stops paying attention to the ring or spends too much time swimming around and biting the ring, give it a brief timeout. Remove the ring from the tank and move away from the tank where the fish cannot see you for a minute or so.

After a week or so, when the fish is retrieving or swimming through the large ring fairly reliably, it is time to switch to a smaller ring. This ring should be made exactly like the first one but slightly smaller (figure 8). The fish, as usual, will notice the difference in rings, and it will be reluctant to stick its head in the ring. To get around this problem, alternate your trials between the small and large ring; you won't need the small hoop anymore. Continue this training until the fish is retrieving the ring reliably (figure 9). Eventually the fish will learn that even if it swims into the ring while facing away from you it has to turn around with the ring and swim back to you if it is going to be fed for its behavior.

It will probably take four to six weeks to train the fish so that it retrieves the ring reliably. It's a good idea to continue to use the larger ring on every other or every second retrieval.

The fish can be trained to retrieve rings floating at the surface and sitting on the bottom if you wish (figure 10). This is more difficult to do than the retrieval from mid-water. To train for surface retrieval, make a ring identical to the small one you have been using but with a large-enough float that it stays at the surface (figure 8). Start training using the small ring suspended at mid-water, and gradually shorten the thread holding the ring until the fish retrieves the ring near the surface. Then substitute the floating ring. Use the same procedure for training to retrieve a ring setting on the bottom, but lengthen the thread instead of shortening it. The fish will not want to pick the ring up directly off the bottom, so a ring with a pair of short legs, as shown in figure 8, must be made. Again make two rings the same sizes as the ones used above, suspended by thread from floats (figure 8).

How are you doing with your notes? Have you had to check your notes to see how long it has been taking you to train a behavior? I hope you are beginning to understand the importance of keeping good records of your work and understand why professional dolphin trainers need to keep good notes.

Figure 9. Fish retrieving ring suspended from float by thread.

Figure 10. Above: fish retrieving floating ring. Below: fish retrieving small sinking ring.

11
Stimulus Control

The fish's behavior is said to be under "stimulus control" when it performs a behavior only when you signal it to do so. You see this at all dolphin shows. The trainer is usually standing on a stage with one or more dolphins "stationing" nearby, watching the trainer. Remember "stationing" is when the dolphin or fish stays at the side of the tank near you. In order to keep them in one place, you can have them stay in contact with the spoon or your finger. It will be necessary to feed them to condition them to do this for extended periods. With the dolphin stationing, the trainer waves his or her arm or gives the animal an underwater sound signal; the dolphin then jumps through a hoop or does some other trick. But it only does the behavior after it has been signaled to do so.

You can have the fish do some of its tricks under stimulus control or on your signal too. Teach the fish to station touching the spoon, drop the ring in the tank, remove the spoon, and wave your hand over the tank and remove the spoon. Of course the fish will not know what this means, but it will see the ring after a few seconds and retrieve it for you. Eventually the fish will learn what your hand wave means and respond more quickly to your signal. You can get other of the tricks you have trained under stimulus control too if you wish and want to spend the time on it.

12

Conclusions

If you have been successful in training your fish to do some or all the behaviors described here, congratulations! Did you get angry at the fish? It's difficult not to sometimes, but keeping your self-control is very important when training animals. Animals are very sensitive to the behavior of other animals, including people.

You should, by now, have some appreciation for the skill and patience of professional animal trainers and be aware of how much planning is necessary before a trainer even starts to train a certain behavior. Think of the planning needed to train a difficult behavior, such as having two dolphins carrying a trainer around a tank, one foot on each one's back. This is called "the chariot ride."

Dolphins are much more intelligent than goldfish but not necessarily much easier to train, at least on the simple behaviors described in this book. There is a big difference in intelligence and trainability. Cats are more intelligent than goldfish, but they are much more difficult to train.

I hope you have enjoyed learning some of the basic principles of animal training and have learned something about yourself too.